CHILL
OUT

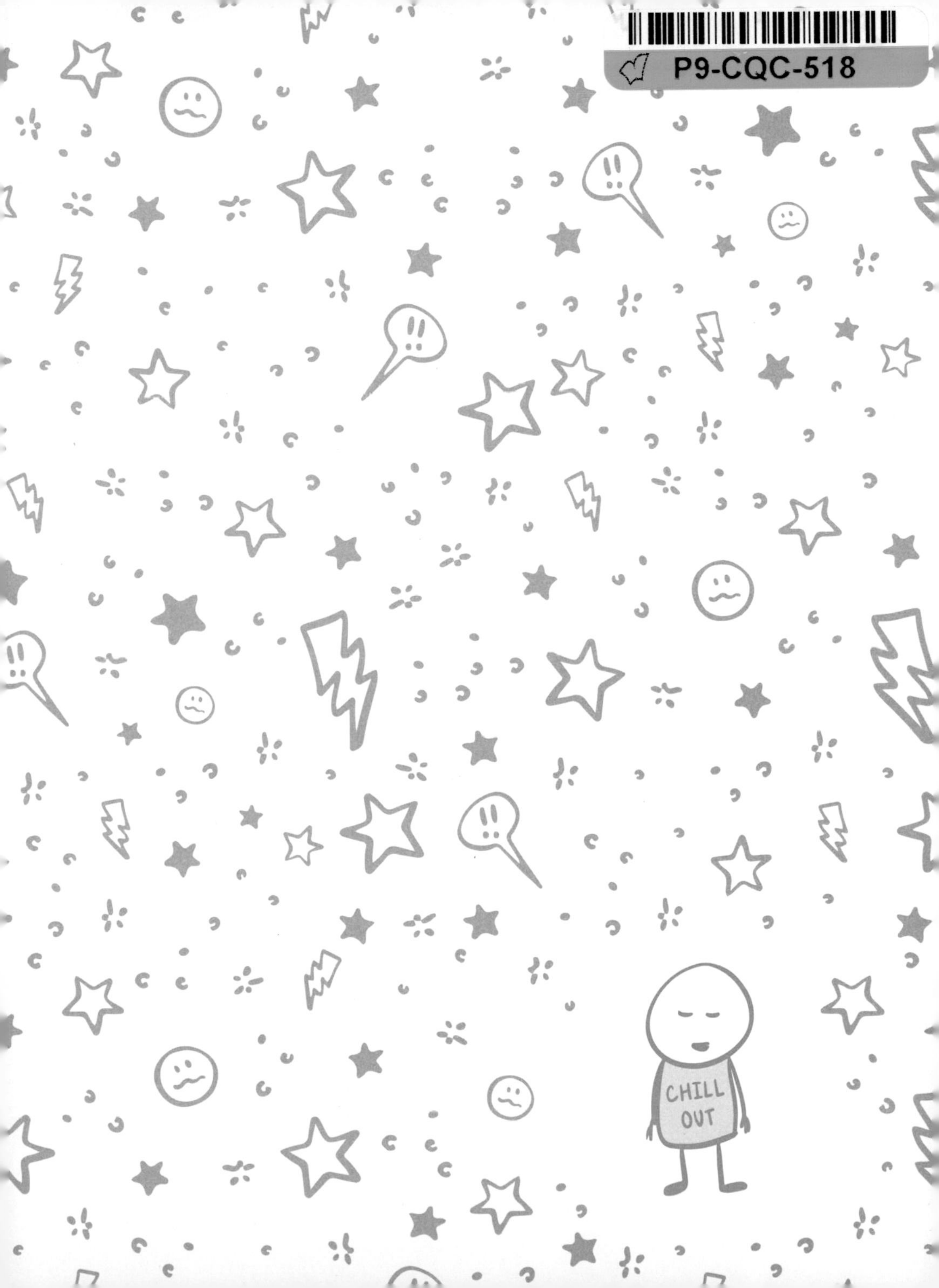

THE WORRY (LESS) BOOK

FEEL STRONG, FIND CALM, AND TAME YOUR ANXIETY!

SEE YOU LATER!

RACHEL BRIAN

L B

LITTLE, BROWN AND COMPANY

NEW YORK   BOSTON

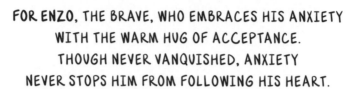

FOR ENZO, THE BRAVE, WHO EMBRACES HIS ANXIETY
WITH THE WARM HUG OF ACCEPTANCE.
THOUGH NEVER VANQUISHED, ANXIETY
NEVER STOPS HIM FROM FOLLOWING HIS HEART.

About This Book

The illustrations for this book were rendered digitally. This book was edited by Lisa Yoskowitz and designed by Jenny Kimura. The production was supervised by Erika Schwartz, and the production editor was Annie McDonnell. The text was set in ConsentforKids, and the display type is hand-lettered.

Little, Brown and Company
Hachette Book Group
1290 Avenue of the Americas, New York, NY 10104
Visit us at LBYR.com

First Edition: September 2020

Little, Brown and Company is a division of Hachette Book Group, Inc.
The Little, Brown name and logo are trademarks of Hachette Book Group, Inc.

The publisher is not responsible for websites (or their content) that are not owned by the publisher.

Library of Congress Control Number: 2019954828

ISBNs: 978-0-316-49519-6 (hardcover), 978-0-316-49517-2 (ebook), 978-0-316-49515-8 (ebook), 978-0-316-49518-9 (ebook) I Printed in China I APS I 10 9 8 7 6 5 4 3 2 1

WELCOME!

THIS BOOK IS FOR PEOPLE WHO WORRY.
SO, YEAH—EVERYONE!

WHAT THIS BOOK **CAN** DO:

EXPLAIN HOW YOUR BODY REACTS TO WORRIES.

AM I SICK?

(NOPE.)

HELP YOU RECOGNIZE ANXIETY.

THERE IT IS!

Ahh...

GIVE YOU IDEAS FOR CALMING YOURSELF.

WHAT IT **CAN'T** DO:

TELL YOU **HOW TO** WORRY.

THAT COMES NATURALLY.

PICK UP YOUR DIRTY SOCKS.

NO WAY!

MAKE ALL ANXIETY DISAPPEAR.

BUMMER.

3

WAIT, WHAT'S ANXIETY?

ANXIETY IS A FEELING,

JUST LIKE

JOY OR ANGER OR HOPE

IT'S THE FEELING OF BEING

Aaah!

WORRIED, NERVOUS, OR AFRAID.

ANXIETY CAN ALERT US TO A THREAT.

LOOK OUT!

THANKS!

DANGER!

ANXIETY

BUT IT CAN ALSO FEEL VERY **UNCOMFORTABLE!**

UGH.

ANXIETY

SO WHETHER YOU HAVE

A LITTLE ANXIETY ABOUT A FEW THINGS (OR) A LOT OF ANXIETY ABOUT A WHOLE HEAP OF THINGS,

THIS BOOK IS HERE TO HELP YOU

UNDERSTAND YOUR ANXIETY

RECOGNIZE IT'S A NORMAL PART OF LIFE

FIND TOOLS TO FEEL CALMER

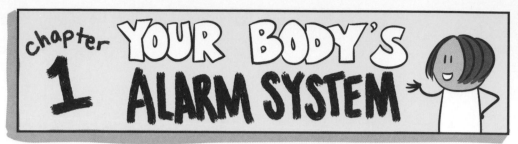

chapter 1 YOUR BODY'S ALARM SYSTEM

EVERYONE HAS A MIX OF FUN
& NOT-SO-FUN FEELINGS EACH DAY:

7:00 TOOTHPASTE EXPLODES — GRR. — **ANNOYED**

9:00 FRIENDS! — **EXCITED**

1:00 QUIZ — OOO OH NO.. — **STRESSED**

3:00 SOCCER — **CONFIDENT**

& EVERYONE

FEELS ANXIOUS SOMETIMES.

I'M ANXIOUS RIGHT NOW!

ANXIETY IS LIKE YOUR BODY'S OWN ALARM SYSTEM—IT ALERTS YOU TO DANGER.

SOMETIMES THE ALARM GOES OFF BECAUSE YOUR BRAIN **PREDICTS** THAT A SITUATION MIGHT BE DANGEROUS.

THERE ARE DIFFERENT WAYS ANXIETY SHOWS UP...

YOU MIGHT FEEL:

UNEASY
(GENERALLY LIKE THINGS AREN'T OK)

FEARFUL
(AFRAID SOMETHING IS DANGEROUS)

NERVOUS
(RESTLESS, JUMPY, ON EDGE)

WORRIED
(OCCUPIED WITH IMAGINING FUTURE PROBLEMS)

STRESSED
(TENSE & OVERWHELMED)

PANICKED
(SUDDENLY INTENSELY FEARFUL)

THOUGH IT MIGHT NOT ALWAYS BE WELCOME, SOME ANXIETY CAN BE HELPFUL:

THE PREDICTIONS YOUR BRAIN MAKES CAN KEEP YOU SAFE.

BUT **TOO MUCH** ANXIETY CAN GET IN THE WAY:

| SUNDAY | MONDAY | TUESDAY | WEDNESDAY | THURSDAY | FRIDAY |

SOME ANXIETIES AREN'T HELPFUL...

I'M AFRAID OF SNOW!

ESPECIALLY IF THE THING YOU'RE WORRIED ABOUT ISN'T REALLY A PROBLEM.

BUT WE LIVE ON A TROPICAL ISLAND!

GOOD POINT. BUT I STILL FEEL WORRIED.

OK, SO I'M NOT PERFECT!

SOMETIMES ANXIETY DOESN'T HAVE A FOCUS. THERE'S NOTHING IN PARTICULAR YOU'RE WORRIED ABOUT.

OTHER TIMES, THERE'S A CAUSE FOR YOUR ANXIETY, BUT YOU'RE JUST NOT SURE WHAT IT IS.

YOU DON'T GET TO PICK WHAT YOU WORRY ABOUT, OR WHEN.

SOME PEOPLE NATURALLY WORRY MORE STRONGLY OR MORE OFTEN THAN OTHER PEOPLE.

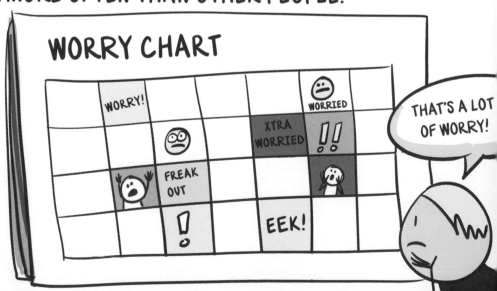

AND HOW MUCH ANXIETY YOU FEEL GOES UP AND DOWN.

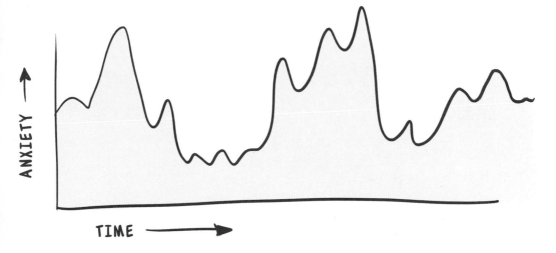

BUT THERE'S NO "RIGHT" OR "WRONG" AMOUNT.

NEWS FLASH!

OCCASIONALLY, PEOPLE FEEL A STRONG, SUDDEN FEELING OF ANXIETY CALLED **PANIC.**

I'VE HAD THAT!

IT MIGHT BE A SENSE OF OVERWHELMING DREAD,

Gulp

OR IT MIGHT FEEL TOTALLY PHYSICAL.

OW! CHEST PAIN!

BUT DON'T WORRY— EVEN REALLY POWERFUL FEELINGS LIKE PANIC WON'T HURT YOU PHYSICALLY.

IT'S JUST A WHOLE BUNCH OF ME!

chapter 2
GUESS WHO?
IT'S ME, ANXIETY

Helloooo!!

IF YOU AREN'T SURE WHAT THEY ARE,
ANXIOUS FEELINGS CAN BE UNSETTLING.

EEK!

BUT WHEN YOU CAN RECOGNIZE YOUR ANXIETY—
IT'S NOT SO SCARY.

OH, HI. YOU AGAIN.

HI!

JUST A SHADOW

HI, MY NAME IS anxiety

SOMETIMES ANXIETY SHOWS UP IN YOUR
THOUGHTS,

ESPECIALLY IF YOU'RE WORRIED ABOUT A SPECIFIC EVENT.

BUT SOME THOUGHTS ARE FREQUENT, INTENSE & DON'T GO AWAY AFTER A STRESSFUL EXPERIENCE.

SOMETIMES ANXIETY SHOWS UP IN THE WAY YOU FEEL.

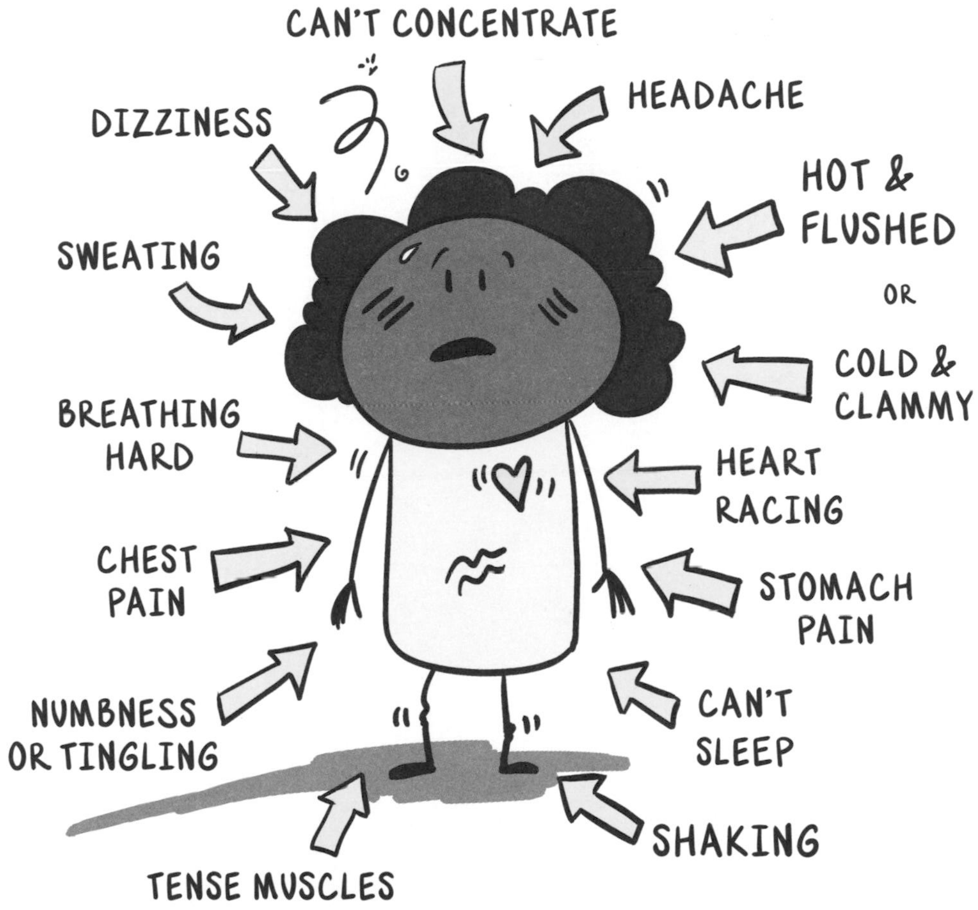

YOU MIGHT FEEL ONE, NONE, OR ALL OF THESE!

SCIENCE CORNER

WHAT ANXIETY DOES IN YOUR **BODY**

FIRST
YOUR BODY RELEASES
ADRENALINE
(A STRESS HORMONE).

ZING!

IT MAKES YOU BREATHE FASTER & QUICKENS YOUR HEART RATE. IT'S GREAT IF YOU NEED TO FLEE FROM AN ANGRY RACCOON!

AAAH!

I JUST WANTED SOME SPAGHETTI!

BUT IT'S NOT GREAT IF YOU'RE TRYING TO FEEL CALM OR FALL ASLEEP.

BREATHING FASTER

HEART POUNDING

MUSCLES READY TO GO!

ANXIETY CAN MAKE YOU FEEL LIKE SOMETHING IS **TERRIBLY WRONG...**

WHO ME?! SORRY ABOUT THAT!

FEELING ANXIOUS?

YEAH! IT'S **SCARY**!

THAT'S YOUR BODY'S NATURAL RESPONSE. IT FEELS AWFUL, BUT YOU'RE OK!

I'M OK? WHEW!

BUT KNOW THAT THE BAD FEELING WILL GO AWAY WITH TIME.

YAY! WAIT... HOW MUCH TIME?

WELL, I'VE GOT LUNCH PLANS AT 1:00...

SOMETIMES JUST KNOWING YOUR ANXIETY IS TEMPORARY & NOT DANGEROUS CAN HELP.

I KNOW I'M GOING TO BE FINE.

TIME

Ahhh...

BECAUSE THE LAST THING YOU NEED TO WORRY ABOUT IS WORRYING!

(YOU DON'T WANT TO GET STUCK IN A WORRY LOOP.)

WORRIED!
OH NO! I SHOULDN'T WORRY!
DO I WORRY TOO MUCH?
THAT MAKES ME EVEN MORE WORRIED!

PEOPLE HAVE LOTS OF
REACTIONS
TO ANXIETY:

UPSET!? I'M NOT UPSET!

YOU DEFINITELY SEEM UPSET.

GETTING ANGRY

IF YOU NOTICE THESE, I MIGHT BE THERE TOO.

ANXIETY

bip bloop bip

NEEDING DISTRACTION

UGH. IT'S NEVER GOOD ENOUGH!

REDOING WORK

IS IT OK?!?

YUP.

ARE YOU SURE?

YES.

REALLY?

CRAVING REASSURANCE

MUNCH MUNCH

BAG O' SNACK

EATING WHEN NOT HUNGRY

I FEEL GROSS—I SHOULD PROBABLY STAY HOME AGAIN.

AVOIDING DAILY LIFE

OW. MY STOMACH ALWAYS HURTS!

FEELING SICK

WHATEVER.

TRYING NOT TO CARE ABOUT ANYTHING.

THE MORE YOU CAN RECOGNIZE ANXIETY...
(IN ALL ITS DISGUISES)

THE MORE YOU CAN DEAL WITH IT DIRECTLY WHEN YOU'RE READY TO.

NEWS FLASH

YOU MIGHT BE WONDERING:

> IF ANXIETY IS NATURAL & USEFUL, WHY DO I HAVE SO MANY UNHELPFUL WORRIES?

WELL, WHILE NATURE HAS CREATED MANY COOL & USEFUL ADAPTATIONS LIKE:

EYES — SEEING IS GREAT!

FUR COATS — I'M CUTE AND TOASTY!

OPPOSABLE THUMBS — I CAN OPEN A JAR!

SOME NATURAL THINGS CAN MAKE LIFE A BIT TOUGHER:

DEER BEHAVIOR ON HIGHWAYS — MESMERIZING!

THE APPENDIX — OW! MY APPENDIX!

MOTH NAVIGATION — OH NO! I'M FLYING INTO THAT CANDLE AGAIN!

SO...YEAH—
YOUR ANXIETY IS NATURAL, BUT IT CAN ALSO BE CHALLENGING.

chapter 3

WORRY in the WAY

NOW YOU KNOW HOW TO **RECOGNIZE** ANXIETY.
(GOOD JOB!)

NOW IT'S TIME TO FIGURE OUT IF IT'S **IN YOUR WAY.**

HOW DO YOU KNOW IF ANXIETY IS CAUSING A PROBLEM?

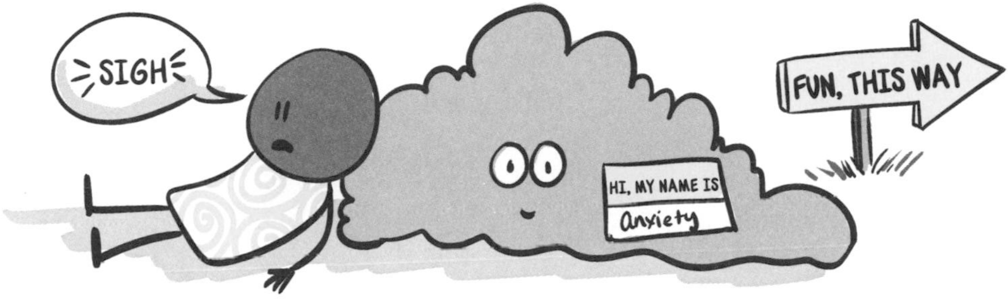
SIGH
FUN, THIS WAY
HI, MY NAME IS
Anxiety

ASK YOURSELF:
AM I DOING WHAT'S IMPORTANT TO ME?

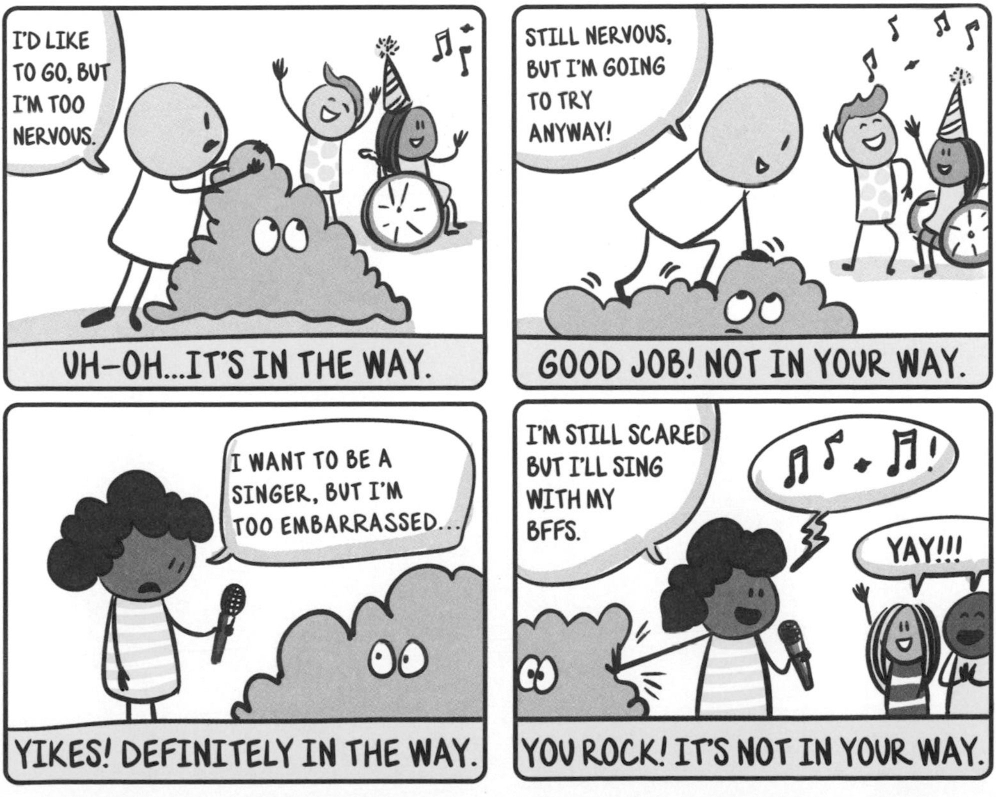
I'D LIKE TO GO, BUT I'M TOO NERVOUS.
UH-OH...IT'S IN THE WAY.
STILL NERVOUS, BUT I'M GOING TO TRY ANYWAY!
GOOD JOB! NOT IN YOUR WAY.
I WANT TO BE A SINGER, BUT I'M TOO EMBARRASSED...
YIKES! DEFINITELY IN THE WAY.
I'M STILL SCARED BUT I'LL SING WITH MY BFFS.
YAY!!!
YOU ROCK! IT'S NOT IN YOUR WAY.

IF YOU'RE FEELING A LOT OF ANXIETY,
A LOT OF THE TIME—IT CAN BE HARD TO DO
THE THINGS YOU WANT TO.

YOU MIGHT FIND IT'S CAUSING PROBLEMS WITH

SLEEP

OR **SCHOOL**

OR **FRIENDSHIPS**

ONE OF THE BEST WAYS TO TELL IF ANXIETY IS A PROBLEM FOR YOU IS TO LOOK AT WHAT YOU

IF YOU'RE AVOIDING THINGS LIKE:

THEN YOU MIGHT BE EXPERIENCING A LOT OF ANXIETY.

THE FARTY PARTY

A MINI COMIC ABOUT "WHAT IF"?

SOMETIMES THE WORST THING IMAGINABLE TURNS OUT TO BE NO BIG DEAL.

chapter 4 FEEL LIKE POO? TAKE CARE of YOU!

YEAH!

IF ANXIETY IS GETTING YOU DOWN, YOU MIGHT NEED SOME TOOLS TO CALM YOURSELF & HELP YOU GET UNSTUCK.

THESE TOOLS CAN GO IN YOUR ANXIETY TOOLBOX.

LIKE THESE?

UH, NO. NOT LITERAL TOOLS.

STRATEGIES TO HELP YOU FEEL OK EVEN WHEN YOU HAVE ANXIETY!

IDEAS THIS WAY

START WITH
THE BASICS.

OK, YOU'RE FEELING NOT GREAT.

BUT THERE MAY BE A FEW THINGS THAT CAN HELP.

YOUR BODY IS A BIT LIKE A HOUSEPLANT.

IT IS?

YEP.

IF YOU TAKE CARE OF PLANTS,
THEY DO PRETTY WELL:

AND IF YOU DON'T,
THEY DON'T DO SO WELL.

IT'S THE SAME THING WITH YOUR BODY.

IT NEEDS SOME BASIC THINGS TO FEEL GOOD. AND WITHOUT THOSE THINGS...

EVERYONE IS DIFFERENT WHEN IT COMES TO WHAT MAKES THEM FEEL GOOD.

BUT WHEN YOU FEEL BAD, ASK YOURSELF:

COULD I FEEL BETTER IF I TOOK TIME TO...

SCIENCE CORNER

WHY DO SIMPLE THINGS SOMETIMES HELP?

WHEN YOU'RE TIRED, HUNGRY, THIRSTY, TOO HOT, OR TOO COLD, YOUR BODY CAN TELL SOMETHING'S OFF.

ALERT!

THAT TRIGGERS YOUR BRAIN'S ALARM SYSTEM.

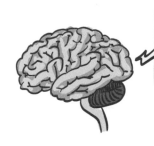

BEGIN OPERATION FREAK-OUT!

Ahh.

IF YOU CAN SOOTHE YOUR BODY A BIT, SOMETIMES YOUR BRAIN CAN RELAX TOO.

FALSE ALARM? COOL! LET'S CHILL.

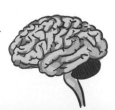

WANTED

FOR MAKING ANXIETY WORSE

CAFFEINE   TOO MUCH SUGAR   LOADS OF SCREEN TIME

BEWARE OF THIS NOTORIOUS GANG!

THE **REWARD** FOR LIMITING YOUR CONTACT WITH THESE CULPRITS—

FEELING MORE RELAXED.

OK, SO IF YOU'VE DONE ALL THAT AND YOU STILL FEEL ANXIOUS...

IT'S TIME TO LOOK AT SOME SPECIFIC TOOLS TO HELP CALM & RELAX YOU.

chapter 5

TRAIN YOUR BRAIN

SIT. STAY! GOOD BRAIN!

OK, YOU CAN'T REALLY CONTROL YOUR BRAIN.

BRAIN, FORGET THAT EMBARRASSING INCIDENT WITH THE UNDERWEAR.

NOPE.

STOP BEING ANXIOUS RIGHT NOW!

UH-UH.

HAVE ONLY HAPPY EMOTIONS!

NOT GONNA DO IT.

JUST LIKE YOU CAN'T CONTROL A LOT OF WHAT YOUR BODY DOES.

STOP THAT DIGESTING RIGHT NOW.

NO SWEATING!

BUT WHEN YOU'RE KNEE-DEEP IN ANXIETY, THERE ARE SOME THINGS YOU CAN DO THAT MAY HELP YOUR MIND & BODY GET BACK IN **BALANCE.**

THEY'RE STRATEGIES YOU CAN KEEP IN YOUR ANXIETY **TOOLBOX...**

SOME ARE WAYS TO CALM YOURSELF WHEN YOUR ANXIETY IS HIGH. OTHERS ARE IDEAS FOR STAYING RESILIENT & STRONG.

TOOL #1
BREATHING

FOCUS ON THE FEELING OF YOUR BREATH AS IT GOES IN AND OUT.

ANXIETY IS LIKE THE **GAS** PEDAL.

BREATHING FASTER

RELEASES ADRENALINE!

SPEEDS UP HEART RATE!

MORE NERVOUS & JITTERY

SLOW BREATHING IS LIKE THE **BRAKES.**

STIMULATES THE VAGUS NERVE (THAT'S GOOD!)

Ahhh.

HEART RATE SLOWS

CALMER & MORE RELAXED

41

TOOL #2
GROUNDING YOUR BODY

START

NOTICE 5 THINGS YOU SEE.

LIKE... • THE WINDOW
• YELLOW RUG
• MY HANDS
• A FLY
• OLD BAND-AID

NOTICE 1 THING YOU TASTE

• TODAY'S SANDWICH (TUNA!)

NOTICE 4 THINGS YOU CAN TOUCH.

• A PILLOW
• THE GROUND UNDER ME
• THE AIR
• SAME OLD BAND-AID

NOTICE 2 THINGS YOU SMELL.

• A PENCIL
• MY SOCKS (EW!)

• A CRICKET
• MY BREATHING
• SOMEONE BURPING

NOTICE 3 THINGS YOU HEAR.

HOW IT WORKS:

WHEN YOU'RE ANXIOUS, YOUR MIND MAY BE AGITATED OR HAVE UNSETTLING THOUGHTS.

WHEN YOU FOCUS ON YOUR BODY & SENSES INSTEAD, IT GIVES YOUR MIND A CHANCE TO QUIET DOWN.

THANKS FOR THE BREAK!

TOOL #3
KEEP A WORRY JOURNAL

WRITE DOWN ALL THE THINGS YOU'RE WORRIED ABOUT.

YOU CAN SHARE YOUR LIST WITH A SUPPORTIVE FRIEND OR ADULT.

YOU CAN EVEN PLAN TO LOOK AT YOUR WORRIES LATER. SOMETIMES THAT CAN HELP YOU RELAX.

TO THINK ABOUT TOMORROW

HOW IT WORKS:

WHEN YOU LOOK RIGHT AT THEM, THE WORRIES DON'T SEEM AS SCARY.

HI THERE.

YO.

TOOL #4 MUSCLE RELAXATION

1 LIE DOWN & BREATHE SLOWLY.

2 STARTING WITH YOUR TOES— SQUEEZE THEM AS HARD AS YOU CAN FOR 10 SECONDS.

THEN LET THEM RELAX FOR 10 SECONDS.

3 MOVE YOUR WAY UP YOUR BODY, SQUEEZING EACH MUSCLE AS HARD AS YOU CAN & THEN LETTING IT RELAX.

4 DON'T FORGET YOUR BELLY, EYELIDS & EVERYTHING IN BETWEEN! (YES, EVEN YOUR BUTT!)

HOW IT WORKS:

WHEN YOU'RE ANXIOUS, YOUR MUSCLES ARE OFTEN TIGHT & TENSE. DOING THIS ACTIVITY MAKES EACH MUSCLE GROUP RELAX.

CHILL OUT

TOOL #5
VISUALIZATION

IF YOUR MIND IS RACING WITH
UNCOMFORTABLE THOUGHTS,
TRY IMAGINING YOURSELF IN A
RELAXING PLACE.

WHAT DOES IT LOOK LIKE?

WHAT DOES IT SOUND LIKE?

WHAT DOES IT FEEL LIKE?

WHAT DOES IT SMELL LIKE?

HOW IT WORKS:

WHEN YOU IMAGINE SOMETHING,
YOUR BRAIN INTERPRETS IT AS THOUGH IT'S
REAL. THINKING ABOUT A RELAXING PLACE
HELPS YOUR BRAIN RELAX TOO.

TOOL #6

CHALLENGING NEGATIVE THOUGHTS

JUST BECAUSE YOU HAVE A THOUGHT... DOESN'T MAKE IT TRUE.

WE'RE DOOMED! DOOMED, I TELL YOU!

WE'RE FINE, REALLY!

SO WHEN YOU HAVE A NEGATIVE THOUGHT, ASK YOURSELF TWO QUESTIONS:

1 HOW LIKELY IS IT TO HAPPEN?

2 WHAT'S THE WORST THAT COULD HAPPEN & HOW WOULD I HANDLE IT?

HOW IT WORKS:

KNOWING YOUR WORRY IS PROBABLY UNLIKELY—AND KNOWING THAT YOU'D BE ABLE TO HANDLE WHATEVER HAPPENS ANYWAY—CAN LESSEN ANXIETY & GIVE YOU CONFIDENCE.

THOSE 6 TOOLS MIGHT HELP YOU GET UNSTUCK WHEN YOU'RE FEELING ANXIOUS.

HERE ARE A COUPLE OF OTHER TOOLS YOU CAN USE EVERY DAY!

EXERCISE!

7 30 MINUTES OF EXERCISE EACH DAY CAN HELP YOUR BODY MANAGE ANXIETY.

8 TALKING WITH SUPPORTIVE PEOPLE WHO CARE ABOUT YOU

HELP.

I GOT YOU!

← GOOD LISTENER

CONNECTING

UNPLUGGING

TAKING A BREAK FROM SCREENS TO BE IN NATURE OR JUST RELAX **9**

chapter 6 GET OUT OF THE ZONE

YOUR COMFORT ZONE, THAT IS!

YOUR COMFORT ZONE IS THE FAMILIAR, RELAXED PART OF YOUR LIFE.

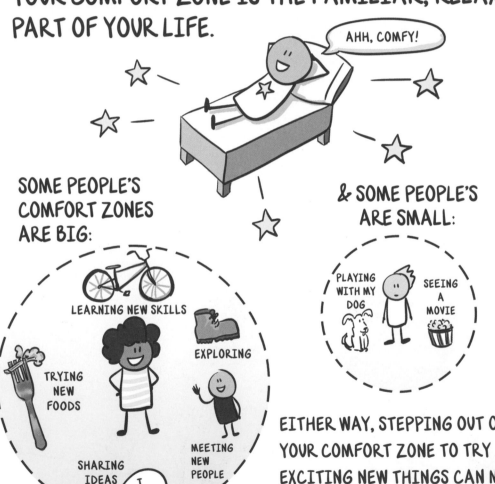

AHH, COMFY!

SOME PEOPLE'S COMFORT ZONES ARE BIG:

LEARNING NEW SKILLS

EXPLORING

TRYING NEW FOODS

SHARING IDEAS

I THINK...

MEETING NEW PEOPLE

& SOME PEOPLE'S ARE SMALL:

PLAYING WITH MY DOG

SEEING A MOVIE

EITHER WAY, STEPPING OUT OF YOUR COMFORT ZONE TO TRY EXCITING NEW THINGS CAN MAKE LIFE MORE FUN AND REWARDING!

STEPPING OUT OF YOUR COMFORT ZONE CAN BE, WELL, **UNCOMFORTABLE.**

BUT USING THE TOOLS IN YOUR TOOLBOX CAN HELP YOU TAKE THE LEAP.

THE BEST WAY TO GROW YOUR COMFORT ZONE...

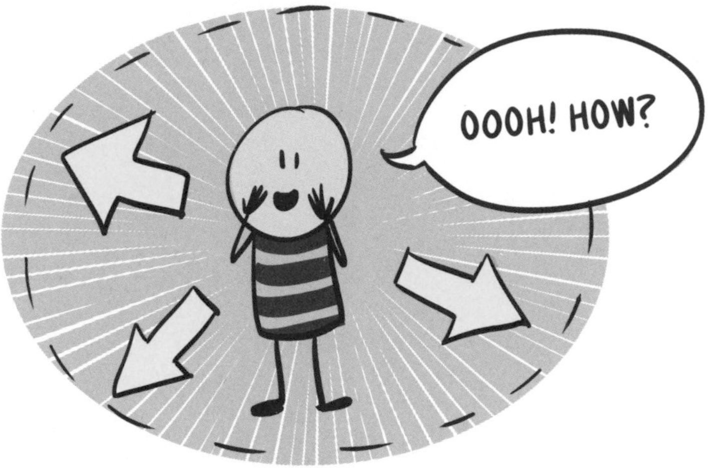
OOOH! HOW?

IS BY DOING THINGS THAT MAKE YOU **UN**COMFORTABLE.

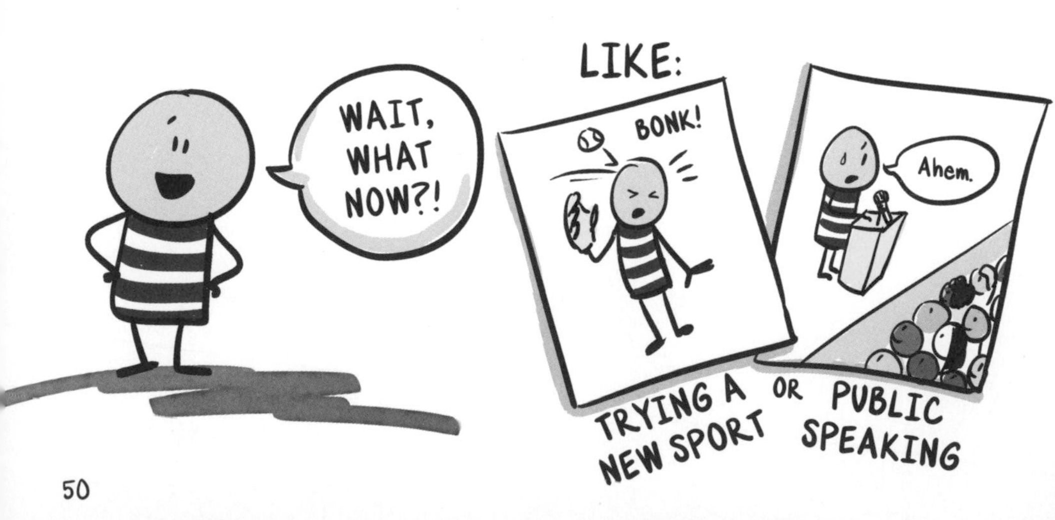
WAIT, WHAT NOW?!
LIKE:
BONK!
Ahem.
TRYING A NEW SPORT
OR
PUBLIC SPEAKING

BECAUSE THE MORE YOU DO SOMETHING, THE MORE YOUR MIND & BODY GET USED TO IT.

THE BETTER YOU GET AT TOLERATING **DISCOMFORT,**

THAT WAS HARD, BUT I TRIED IT & MADE IT THROUGH!
I'M PROUD OF MYSELF.

THE MORE COMFORTABLE YOU'LL BE MOST OF THE TIME.

FEELING CONFIDENT

HARVE THE DOG

A MINI COMIC

HARVE THE DOG WAS CONTENT.

HE LOVED NAPPING ON HIS HUMANS,

ZZZZ

TREATS

& BELLY RUBS

BUT THERE WAS ONE THING HARVE DID **NOT** LIKE...

the **OUTDOORS...**

NO NO NO NO!

C'MON!

THE OUTDOORS WAS FULL OF THINGS THAT WORRIED HARVE...

EEK!

TIPPED OVER FLOWERPOTS

!

?

TRASH CANS

THEY'LL NEVER SEE ME HERE!

?

FRIENDLY OTHER DOGS

ONE DAY, HARVE WAS ALARMED BY A TALL WEED BLOWING IN THE WIND.

BUT EVERY DAY, HARVE WENT OUT. (A DOG'S GOTTA PEE.)

I'LL DO IT!

EVEN THOUGH HE WAS AFRAID,

WHAT'S THIS TERRIBLE WET STUFF?

HE EXPLORED

MMM...GREAT SMELLS!

& HE STARTED TO FEEL LESS AFRAID.

WELL, STILL AFRAID SOMETIMES.

HIDING, YES.

THAT WAS OK, BECAUSE SOMETIMES HE WASN'T AFRAID AT ALL.

HI, WEED!

HIS COMFORT GREW

MMM... I THINK I ATE A BEE! oh well.

& GREW

WHEE!

& HE WAS FREE TO LIVE HIS BEST DOG LIFE.

THE END

chapter 7 FAIL FORWARD

HUH?

THERE ARE LOTS OF THINGS THAT TRIGGER ANXIETY. BUT MANY ANXIETIES HAVE A SIMILAR ROOT—

FEAR OF FAILURE.

EEK!

THE PROBLEM IS, YOU OFTEN HAVE TO FAIL **MANY TIMES** BEFORE YOU SUCCEED AT SOMETHING.

FIRST WORDS

GAC!

FIRST STEPS

WHOA!

FIRST TIME TYING SHOES

FIRST TIME PLAYING BASKETBALL

!

:plunk:

TAKING RISKS

TO LEARN & GROW, SOMETIMES YOU HAVE TO TAKE RISKS.

RISKS? THAT DOESN'T SOUND SAFE!

NOT THE KIND OF RISKS THAT PUT YOU IN MORTAL DANGER.

(NO SWIMMING BLINDFOLDED WITH SHARKS WHILE HOLDING FISH HEADS.)

THE KIND OF RISKS THAT ARE SAFE BUT MIGHT MAKE YOU NERVOUS AT FIRST.

TRYING A NEW FOOD

STUDYING A NEW LANGUAGE

TAKING A DANCE CLASS

LEARNING TO RIDE A BIKE

A LOT OF PEOPLE TRY TO MAKE LIFE LOOK **PERFECT...**

(ESPECIALLY ONLINE)

♥ 750

♥ 1,025

1 MINUTE LATER...

BUT THERE ARE LOTS OF DIFFICULT, ANXIOUS, SAD & EMBARRASSING MOMENTS TOO.

I DEFINITELY DON'T POST THOSE!

WHY DON'T PEOPLE TALK MORE ABOUT **FAILURE?**

WELL, SOMETIMES, UNDER THE PILE OF ANXIETY, THERE'S A BIG WORRY.

WHEN YOU DIG DOWN, YOU'LL FIND IT.

AM I GOOD ENOUGH?

THE GOOD NEWS IS:

YES, YOU **ARE** GOOD ENOUGH!

JUST BY BEING YOU.

EVEN IF YOU ONLY HAVE ONE "LIKE" & IT'S YOUR MOM

OR YOU GOT A BAD GRADE

OR MADE A MISTAKE

BEING IMPERFECT MAKES YOU HUMAN.

IMAGINE IF YOU **COULD** BE PERFECT—THAT WOULD BE SOOO BORING!

LETTING GO OF THE IDEA OF BEING PERFECT CAN LESSEN ANXIETY.

BECAUSE WHEN:

THINGS DON'T GO WELL...

OR SOMEONE IS MAD AT YOU...

OR YOU FEEL WORRIED ABOUT THE PAST OR FUTURE...

WHAT IF?

IT MIGHT HELP TO REMEMBER: DIFFICULT STUFF IS JUST PART OF LIFE! YOU'RE STILL OK.

THIS GRADE ISN'T ME. I JUST NEED MORE PRACTICE.

SOMETIMES I MAKE MISTAKES. WE CAN WORK IT OUT.

IT'S NORMAL TO WORRY. I CAN ALSO THINK OF SOMETHING I'M GRATEFUL FOR.

HERE TO HELP!

IF YOUR ANXIETY IS TOO BIG TO HANDLE ALONE, DON'T KEEP IT TO YOURSELF!

THERE ARE PEOPLE WHO CAN HELP.

THERAPISTS

PSYCHOLOGISTS

& SOMETIMES DOCTORS WHO CAN PRESCRIBE MEDICINE

THERE ARE ALSO LOTS OF RESOURCES:

WEBSITES
NAMI.ORG
AACAP.ORG
ADAA.ORG

I NEED SOME HELP LEARNING TO USE MY TOOLS, AND THAT'S OK!

NEWS FLASH!

NOT EVERYONE SHOWS UNDERSTANDING WHEN A PERSON IS FEELING ANXIOUS...

SOME PEOPLE MIGHT ACT FRUSTRATED, MAKE FUN, OR EVEN GET ANGRY.

HOW TO BE SUPPORTIVE:

- ⭐ LISTEN WITHOUT JUDGING
- ⭐ TRY TO UNDERSTAND
- ⭐ ASK WHAT SUPPORT THEY'D LIKE

REMEMBER, YOU'RE SO MUCH MORE THAN YOUR ANXIETY.

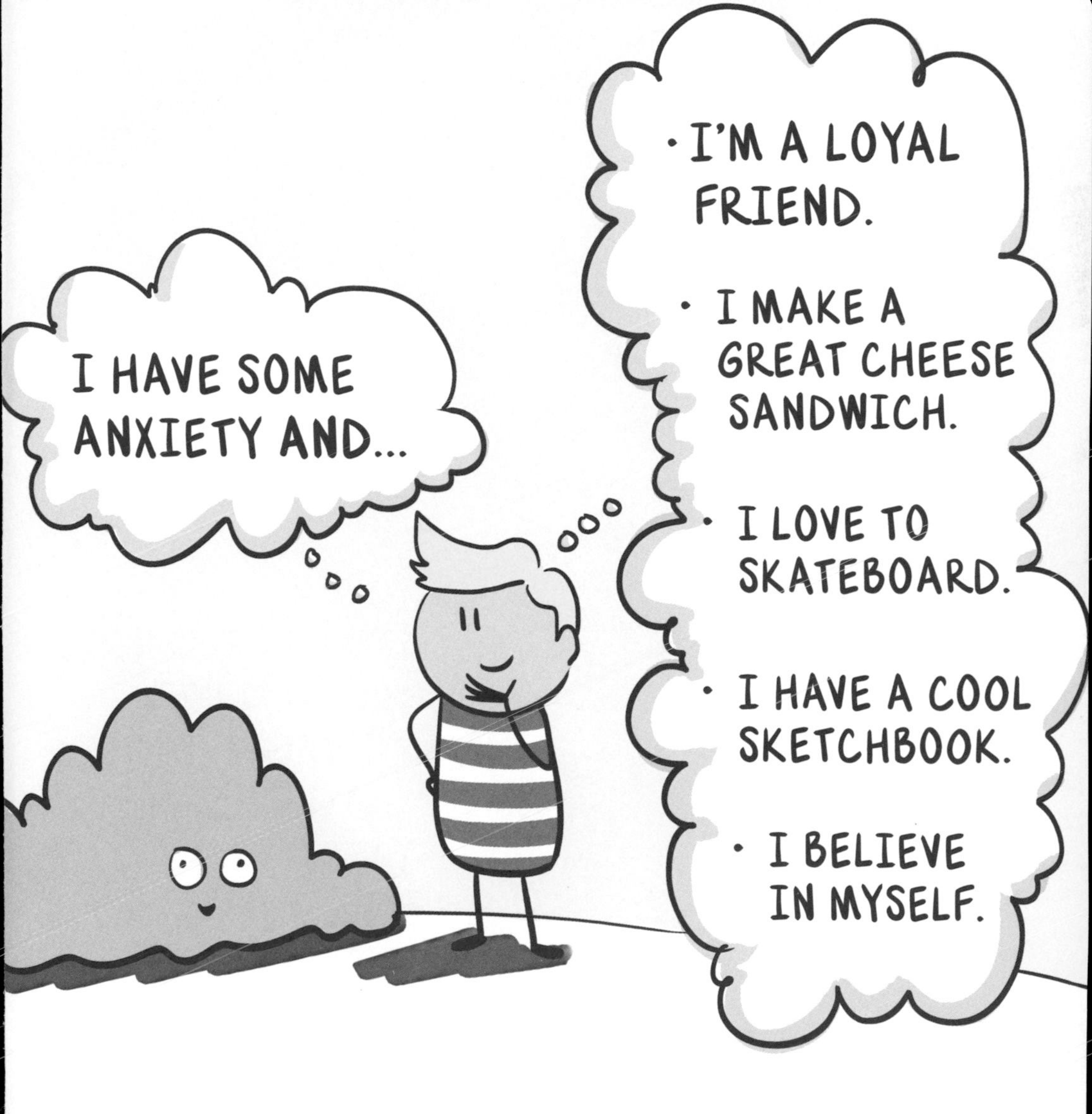

I HAVE SOME ANXIETY AND...
· I'M A LOYAL FRIEND.
· I MAKE A GREAT CHEESE SANDWICH.
· I LOVE TO SKATEBOARD.
· I HAVE A COOL SKETCHBOOK.
· I BELIEVE IN MYSELF.

& EVEN WITH ANXIETY, YOU CAN STILL BE BRAVE.

BEING
BRAVE
DOESN'T MEAN YOU DON'T HAVE FEAR OR ANXIETY...

BRAVERY CAN MEAN DOING WHAT'S
IMPORTANT TO YOU
DESPITE YOUR ANXIETY.

I DID IT!

EVERY CHALLENGE YOU OVERCOME, WHETHER BIG OR SMALL, WILL MAKE YOU STRONGER & MORE CONFIDENT.

ACKNOWLEDGMENTS

Thanks to Lorenzo Battaglia, who has tremendous personal insight into the world of anxiety and who shared many creative ideas. His thoughtful reading and commentary was invaluable.

For Lisa Yoskowitz, my editor, who tamed this book into linear format from a first draft that was more of an impressionist painting. Thanks for all your hard work, and for pushing this book to be such a helpful resource for kids. It's so much stronger for your efforts.

For Laura Horsley, whose smart comments and fantastic title grounded this book.

To Laura Westberg, whose deep understanding and sharp mind came to my rescue as I worked out my ideas on a napkin over platanos maduros.

For my sagacious sis, whose brain and insights I borrow from time to time.

Thanks to Karina Granda and the whole team at Hachette, for making this book so, so beautiful in its final form.

Thanks to Molly Ker Hawn, agent extraordinaire, for being always brilliant.

For Elizabeth Cohen, PhD, cognitive behavior specialist, brilliant clinical psychologist, and incredibly insightful practitioner, for being one of my expert readers, offering fantastic feedback and suggesting important and useful strategies for kids.

For John P. Forsyth, PhD, whose books on Acceptance and Commitment Therapy (ACT) were an inspiration. Thanks for your kind reading of these pages and thoughtful feedback on the ACT aspects. Your work around letting go of the struggle against anxiety was a key underpinning of this book.

For Angela Runder, LICSW, who has an intuitive sense of how children relate to anxiety, for your careful reading and feedback.

To Julie Talbutt, for 40 years of friendship. I'm lucky to know you.

For Lola and Milo Battaglia, you provided me with countless insights about the different ways anxiety can affect kids. Thanks for being so patient with me as I worked on this book. (Sorry about all the pizza!)

For Mike Araujo, who offered equal parts encouragement and distraction. You helped me find the balance and equanimity I needed to wrestle these ideas onto the page.

RACHEL BRIAN

feels anxious now and then, but she's OK with that, because it's just a part of life! She is the founder, owner, and principal animator of Blue Seat Studios, and is best known for her work on *Tea Consent* and the book *Consent (For Kids!)*. A lifelong artist, Rachel is a former researcher and educator. She lives in Rhode Island with a handful of children, a sprinkling of dogs, and her partner.